DEVOTED PRESENCE

A 90-Day Devotional on Living, Loving,
and Leading for Everyday Devotion
Vol III of Holy Habits- The Sacred Year

Angelyna Hawbecker

Sacred Ember Press

Published by Sacred Ember Press
ISBN: 979-8-9999040-4-1

For the ones who stay —
quiet givers, sacred stewards,
those who love with their lives
and speak in your presence more than words.

You remind me that devotion is not loud —
It is lived.

CONTENTS

INTRODUCTION

The soul longs not just to awaken, but to live awake.

Where Shadow to Sacred unlearned old patterns, and Sacred Repatterning built new rhythms, Devoted Presence invites you to embody those rhythms in your daily breath.

This is a book about integration—walking your talk, loving from truth, and leading quietly by example. Presence does not demand perfection; it asks only for attention and devotion. When you are present in your life, you become a living prayer. Take your time. Let each day meet you exactly where you are.

This is not about becoming someone new; it is about becoming fully yourself, here and now.

Devotion is not a destination — it is a way of being.

In this third volume, we turn inward not to heal or to fix, but to live fully. Here, we practice presence. We embody what we believe. We bring our sacred work into the everyday — into meals, movements, moments of service, and quiet moments of prayer.

MESSAGE FROM THE AUTHOR

You are entering the third volume in the devotional
series Holy Habits - The Sacred Year.

Devoted Presence is about anchoring your truth so deeply that
even the smallest actions become an offering.

Across these 90 days, you will explore what it means to live
your values in real time, love without control, lead by
example, and trust the slow, sacred path.

This is the volume of quiet power — of soul integrity, of
honoring your pace, of tending your inner flame.
Let this be your practice. Let this be your devotion.

If you are arriving here after walking through Shadow to
Sacred and Sacred Repatterning, welcome to the anchoring
phase of your journey.

If you are beginning here, know this: you are exactly where
you need to be.

This book is about embodiment—bringing the rhythms you
have learned into daily life. It is about quiet devotion, sacred
presence, and living your truth in every ordinary moment.

Angelyna

WEEK 1: EMBODIED TRUTH —
LIVING WHAT YOU BELIEVE

"Your actions will always tell the truth, even when your words do not." — *Unknown.*

Truth begins not in the words you speak but in the way you move through your ordinary days. Living what you believe is not about making grand declarations or needing to prove yourself; it is the quiet, steady choice to let your actions reflect your deepest values. Integrity doesn't demand perfection; it asks for honesty, moment by moment.

When you rise in the morning and choose patience over rushing, or kindness over irritation, you are already living in integrity. When your outer life echoes what your soul holds dear, you anchor into peace that cannot be shaken by circumstance. The world doesn't always need more talk of truth—it longs to see it lived.

This week invites you to soften into presence. Instead of striving to "get it all right," notice where your life already aligns with what you cherish. Celebrate those moments. Then, gently return to alignment when you drift.

Truth is not a heavy burden; it is the soul's natural way of breathing.

Day 1: The Integrity of Presence

The Hidden Pattern:

Truth begins quietly, not performance. Living what you believe does not require proving anything to anyone. It is alignment—your inner truth reflected in outer action.

The Sacred Reframe:

Integrity is not perfection; it's presence. You do not have to "get it all right" to be true. Every time you choose honesty with yourself, you anchor into soul-alignment.

The Devoted Practice:

Sit with your hand over your heart and whisper: *"I choose to live true."*

Journal: *Where in my life do my actions already align with my beliefs? Where do they feel out of sync?*

Optional: Write one small, aligned action you can take today, no matter how simple.

Day 2: Quiet Truths, Loud Life

The Hidden Pattern:

Truth does not always need to be spoken to be known. Sometimes the loudest truth is how you live when no one is watching.

The Sacred Reframe:

You do not need to convince anyone of who you are. Quiet truth lived daily becomes a light that others feel without explanation.

The Devoted Practice:

Choose one ordinary action today to do with deep presence—washing dishes, walking, printing your name.

Journal: *What simple actions feel most honest to me? What do they say about who I really am?*

Optional: Light a candle and dedicate this quiet truth to someone you love—without ever needing to tell them.

Day 3: The Courage of Alignment

The Hidden Pattern:

It is easier to talk about what you value than to live it. Alignment can feel risky because it asks you to move, not just dream.

The Sacred Reframe:

Courage is not about never wavering; it's about returning to what you know is true, even when it costs you comfort.

The Devoted Practice:

Whisper aloud: *"I choose courage over comfort."*

Journal: *Where have I avoided action because it might feel uncomfortable? What truth is calling me to move anyway?*

Optional: Take one small action that reflects a value you hold dear.

Day 4: Repairing the Gaps

The Hidden Pattern:

When you notice a gap between what you say and how you live, shame is not the answer—repair is. Truth grows in self-compassion, not self-punishment.

The Sacred Reframe:

There is no integrity without grace. You are allowed to acknowledge missteps and choose again. Repair is as sacred as consistency.

The Devoted Practice:

Place your hands over your belly and breathe deeply, saying: *"I allow myself to begin again."*

Journal: *Where have I judged myself for not being consistent? What would gentle repair look like instead?*

Optional: Write a soft apology to yourself, forgiving any old mistakes.

Day 5: Living Without Apology

The Hidden Pattern:

When you live true, some people may not understand—and that is okay. Living authentically means releasing the need for approval.

The Sacred Reframe:

Your truth is not a weapon, nor is it a performance. It is simply who you are. Living without apology is honoring the life you were given, not betraying anyone else's.

The Devoted Practice:

Stand or sit tall and say aloud: *"My truth is sacred."*

Journal: *Where do I still shrink to avoid being misunderstood? What would an unapologetic presence look like for me?*

Optional: Write a short affirmation you can repeat when you feel tempted to dim yourself.

Day 6: Devotion in the Ordinary

The Hidden Pattern:

The truest devotion is not found in grand gestures—it's in how you live daily life. Truth becomes devotion when it's practiced consistently, even in unimportant things.

The Sacred Reframe:

Sacredness lives in how you tie your shoes, how you speak to others, and how you breathe. When you live from truth in the small moments, you are worshipping life itself.

The Devoted Practice:

Whisper: *"My ordinary life is sacred."*

Journal: *What simple daily habits already feel sacred to me? What new one would I like to make sacred?*

Optional: Choose one ordinary action to perform today as a sacred act—pouring tea, folding laundry, breathing deeply.

Day 7: The Blessing of Integrity

The Hidden Pattern:

Integrity is not the absence of mistakes—it's the presence of return. Truth blesses your life every time you return to it, no matter how many times you wander.

The Sacred Reframe:

You are not meant to live perfectly; you are meant to live honestly. Presence is the ultimate prayer.

The Devoted Practice:

Light a candle and whisper: *"I return to what is true, again and again."*

Journal: *How has my relationship with truth shifted this week? What feels different in my body when I live aligned?*

Optional: Write a short blessing to yourself for choosing to live true, even when it's hard.

WEEK 2: SACRED CONSISTENCY — DEVOTION IN THE EVERYDAY

"What you do every day matters more than what you do once in a while." – Gretchen Rubin.

Consistency may feel ordinary, even dull at times, yet it is the most fertile ground for transformation. Just as water carves stone through persistence, your daily practice shapes your soul far more than any rare surge of effort.

What you return to again and again becomes the rhythm of your becoming.

Devotion is not measured in grand gestures but in the quiet return—the breath you take when you pause to pray, the way you light a candle, the habit of coming back to your journal when you've fallen away. Each return is holy. Each act tells your soul: "I am willing to begin again."

This week, notice where do you keep showing up, even when it doesn't feel extraordinary.

Let this steady devotion remind you that change takes root slowly, but surely. Returning itself is devotion.

Day 1: The Power of Repetition

The Hidden Pattern:

Consistency can feel ordinary, but it is the soil where transformation takes root. Repeated small acts create sacred grooves in the soul.

The Sacred Reframe:

Your devotion is not measured by intensity, but by return. Every time you come back to your practice, you are rewriting your story.

The Devoted Practice:

Whisper: *"Returning is devotion."*

Journal: *What small act has been quietly changing me over time? What would I like to nurture more consistently?*

Optional: Light a candle in the morning each day this week as a simple returning ritual.

Day 2: Gentle Rhythm, Not Rigid Rules

The Hidden Pattern:

Consistency is not about harsh rules—it's about rhythm. Sacred habits should feel like breathing, not punishment.

The Sacred Reframe:

You are not here to prove worthiness through perfect discipline. You are here to create sacred flow that nourishes you.

The Devoted Practice:

Breathe deeply and whisper: *"My rhythm is holy."*

Journal: *Where have I confused devotion with pressure? What would consistency that feels kind look like?*

Optional: Identify one practice you can soften—make it feel nourishing, not forced.

Day 3: Choosing Presence
Over Perfection

The Hidden Pattern:

A missed day does not erase your devotion. Presence is not perfection—it's coming back without shame.

The Sacred Reframe:

The moment you return is the moment you are already aligned. You are not starting over; you are continuing.

The Devoted Practice:

Place your hand over your heart and whisper: *"I can always begin again."*

Journal: *Where have I been too harsh with myself for not being perfect? How can I bless my return instead?*

Optional: Light a candle as a symbol of your return to consistency today.

Day 4: Building Sacred Grooves

The Hidden Pattern:

The body learns through repetition. Sacred habits carve gentle grooves in your spirit—paths you can walk even on hard days.

The Sacred Reframe:

You do not need motivation every day. Your soul learns to move in devotion because it remembers the path you've walked before.

The Devoted Practice:

Whisper: *"My soul remembers."*

Journal: *What sacred habit has become easier over time? What new groove am I carving now?*

Optional: Repeat a small ritual today (tea, candle, breath) at the same time as yesterday to deepen the groove.

Day 5: Devotion in the Mundane

The Hidden Pattern:

Folding laundry, stirring soup, brushing teeth, these can all become altars when done with love. Consistency transforms the mundane into sacred.

The Sacred Reframe:

Nothing is too ordinary to hold repeated loving act is prayer in motion. Where you show up consistently is an act of devotion.

The Devoted Practice:

Choose one daily task to perform with intention. Whisper: *"This too is holy."*

Journal: *What ordinary part of my life feels different when I do it with devotion?*

Optional: Write a simple blessing for your home or daily routine.

Day 6: Trusting the Slow Bloom

The Hidden Pattern:

Sacred habits rarely show instant results. Consistency is faith in action—trusting that unseen growth is happening beneath the surface.

The Sacred Reframe:

You are not failing because you can't see change yet. Each consistent act is a seed. Trust the bloom will come in its own time.

The Devoted Practice:

Hold a seed, stone, or small object and whisper: *"I trust what is growing in me."*

Journal: *What feels unseen in my growth right now? How can I trust it more?*

Optional: Water a plant or place a small bowl of water as a symbol of trust in slow growth.

Day 7: The Blessing of Return

The Hidden Pattern:

The greatest gift of consistency is not perfection—it's the ability to return, again and again, with love.

The Sacred Reframe:

Every return is a small resurrection. You rise each time you come back to what matters.

The Devoted Practice:

Light a candle and whisper: *"I bless my return."*

Journal: *What did I learn about myself this week through consistency?*

Optional: Write a blessing to yourself for choosing devotion in the everyday.

WEEK 3: LOVING FROM PRESENCE — QUIET SERVICE AS PRAYER

"The best way to find yourself is to lose yourself in the service of others." – Mahatma Gandhi

Service often gets tangled with striving. It's that desire to fix, to solve, to carry what was never ours. But true service is simpler, quieter, and deeper. It is the way you show up with your whole presence, offering attention without agenda.

It is listening without rushing to answer. It is love embodied in stillness.

Your presence is more healing than you realize. The people around you don't always need your solutions; sometimes they just need your steady being.

Love is not proven in effort—it is revealed in presence. When you sit with someone in silence, when you breathe with them through their pain, you are praying with your life.

This week invites you to trust the power of presence. You don't have to fix. You don't have to prove. Simply being with someone, fully here, can be your deepest gift.

Day 1: Presence Is the Gift

The Hidden Pattern:

You do not need to fix, save, or solve to serve. Sometimes the most sacred gift is simply being fully present. Rescuing isn't the same as be present.

The Sacred Reframe:

Your presence alone can be healing. Love does not need to be loud; it just needs to be real. There is a depth of healing that happens when you offer your presence in places where chaos is trying to reign.

The Devoted Practice:

Whisper: *"My presence is enough."*

Journal: *Who in my life feels loved simply because I am present with them? How can I offer that more often?*

Optional: Sit quietly with someone today—no advice, no agenda, just presence.

Day 2: Listening as Prayer

The Hidden Pattern:

True listening is rare. To listen without planning your response is to hold sacred space for another soul.

The Sacred Reframe:

Every time you listen deeply, you create a sanctuary. Listening is not passive—it is prayer in motion.

The Devoted Practice:

Whisper: *"I create space by listening."*

Journal: *How do I feel when someone listens deeply to me? Who might need that gift from me today?*

Optional: Spend a few minutes in silence, listening to the world around you before speaking to anyone.

Day 3: Quiet Service, Sacred Offering

The Hidden Pattern:

The holiest service often goes unnoticed. You may never know how much your small kindness changes someone's life.

The Sacred Reframe:

Service is not about recognition; it's about love. Every unseen act becomes a prayer whispered into the world.

The Devoted Practice:

Whisper: *"I serve because love asks me to."*

Journal: *How does it feel to love quietly without needing acknowledgment?*

Optional: Do one act of quiet service today, hold a door, send a kind note, wash a dish—without telling anyone.

Day 4: Loving Without Fixing

The Hidden Pattern:

Your role is not always to solve. Trying to fix everything can be a way of avoiding discomfort, not love.

The Sacred Reframe:

Holding space for someone's process is love. Trusting their journey is a deeper prayer than rushing to rescue.

The Devoted Practice:

Whisper: *"I trust their path, and I bless it."*

Journal: *Who am I tempted to "fix," and how can I love them instead by trusting their strength?*

Optional: Light a candle for someone you love and simply hold them in your heart, asking nothing for them but grace.

Day 5: The Sacred Mirror

The Hidden Pattern:

The way you love yourself teaches others how to love themselves. Your presence becomes a mirror when you live kindly toward yourself.

The Sacred Reframe:

Self-compassion is not selfish—it ripples outward. Loving yourself is one of the most generous prayers you can offer.

The Devoted Practice:

Look in a mirror and say: *"The way I treat myself teaches love."*

Journal: *What is one way I can love myself better today so I can love others more fully?*

Optional: Offer yourself a kind gesture—rest, a nourishing meal, a moment of stillness.

Day 6: Boundaries as Sacred Service

The Hidden Pattern:

Loving well requires clear edges. Without boundaries, service turns to resentment.

The Sacred Reframe:

Saying no when needed is also love—it protects your energy so you can give from fullness, not depletion.

The Devoted Practice:

Whisper: *"My no is love too."*

Journal: *Where do I give past my capacity? How might a boundary allow me to love more deeply?*

Optional: Write one loving boundary you'll hold this week, for yourself and for others.

Day 7: Love as a Daily Prayer

The Hidden Pattern:

Love is not just an emotion; it is a rhythm, a devotion you practice every day.

The Sacred Reframe:

Every word, gesture, and breath can become a prayer when offered with love.

The Devoted Practice:

Light a candle and whisper: *"May everything I do be a prayer of love."*

Journal: *What small acts of love felt most sacred this week? How did they shift my presence?*

Optional: Write a blessing to someone in your life, even if you never share it with them.

WEEK 4: SOUL INTEGRITY —
WALKING YOUR TALK

"What you practice, you become." – Unknown

There is a deep ease that settles in the soul when your words and actions match. Integrity is not about flawless living, it is about harmony, about returning to alignment again and again.

When you live what you speak, you strengthen trust in yourself, and others feel it too.

Misalignment feels heavy. Perhaps you've said "yes" when you meant "no," or promised yourself a boundary and then abandoned it. Each misstep is not failure, but an invitation to realign.

The beauty of integrity is that it is always one choice away. You can begin again at any moment.

This week, let your focus be simple: walk your talk in small ways. Say what you mean. Follow through on one quiet promise.

Even the smallest alignment between your inner truth and outer life will ripple peace through your being.

Day 1: The Call of Alignment

The Hidden Pattern:

When your words and actions match, the soul feels peaceful.
When they don't, unease grows. Integrity is not about being
flawless; it's about returning to alignment as often as possible.

The Sacred Reframe:

Your soul longs for harmony between what you say and how you
live. Even small alignments strengthen trust in yourself.

The Devoted Practice:

Whisper: *"I align with what I value."*

Journal: *Where do I feel most at peace because I live aligned?*
Where do I feel unsettled because I don't?

Optional: Take one small action today that matches a
belief you hold deeply.

Day 2: Honoring Your Own Promises

The Hidden Pattern:

We often keep promises to others but break the ones we make ourselves. Integrity begins when you honor your own word.

The Sacred Reframe:

Keeping even the smallest promise to yourself rebuilds self-trust. You are worthy of your own follow-through.

The Devoted Practice:

Whisper: *"I keep promises to myself."*

Journal: *What promise have I been breaking to myself? How can I keep it gently, starting today?*

Optional: Write one simple promise you will keep today and follow through.

Day 3: Integrity Over Image

The Hidden Pattern:

It is tempting to look aligned rather than live aligned. But integrity isn't for show—it's for the soul.

The Sacred Reframe:

You do not need to prove anything to anyone. Your quiet, honest life speaks louder than any performance.

The Devoted Practice:

Whisper: *"I live for truth, not appearance."*

Journal: *Where have I tried to look more aligned than I feel? How can I be more honest with myself instead?*

Optional: Do one act of alignment today that no one else will ever see.

Day 4: The Courage to Correct Course

The Hidden Pattern:

Integrity is not about never straying; it's about noticing when you do and gently correcting course.

The Sacred Reframe:

You are allowed to change your mind, apologize, and begin again. This is not weakness; this is strength.

The Devoted Practice:

Whisper: *"I can always choose again."*

Journal: *Where do I need to realign, and what is one loving step I can take toward it?*

Optional: Write a short apology or forgiveness note—to yourself or someone else—even if you never send it.

Day 5: The Integrity of Saying No

The Hidden Pattern:

Saying yes to everything when your heart says no fractures your integrity. Boundaries protect the truth you're trying to live.

The Sacred Reframe:

A loving no is a sacred yes to your soul. Every time you honor your limits, you walk in deeper truth.

The Devoted Practice:

Whisper: *"My no is holy."*

Journal: *Where have I been saying yes out of guilt or habit? What would integrity look like instead?*

Optional: Practice saying a simple, clear no today, even to something small.

Day 6: Living Small Truths Daily

The Hidden Pattern:

Integrity isn't built in grand gestures; it's built in daily choices. Small truths lived consistently become unshakable foundations.

The Sacred Reframe:

You do not need to overhaul your whole life to walk your talk. One honest choice at a time is enough.

The Devoted Practice:

Whisper: *"Small truths matter."*

Journal: *What small, honest choice can I make today to honor who I really am?*

Optional: Write a list of 3 small truths you're proud to be living.

Day 7: The Peace of Walking True

The Hidden Pattern:

When you walk your talk, the soul rests easier. Integrity may be challenging at times, but it always brings peace.

The Sacred Reframe:

You are not perfect, and you don't need to be. Your consistent return to truth is what makes your life trustworthy.

The Devoted Practice:

Light a candle and whisper: *"I bless my path of truth."*

Journal: *What does peace feel like in my body when I live aligned?*

Optional: Write a short blessing for yourself for choosing integrity again and again.

WEEK 5: GENTLE LEADERSHIP —
INFLUENCE THROUGH EXAMPLE

"Be the change that you wish to see in the world." – Mahatma Gandhi

Leadership is not always loud or commanding. Gentle leadership begins within you—in how you live, how you treat yourself, how you embody what matters most.

The influence of a life quietly lived in alignment often carries more weight than titles or authority ever could.

Think of the people who shaped you most. Were they always the ones with positions of power? Or were they the ones who lived with integrity, who loved with constancy, who modeled a unique way of being?

Influence flows from example more than instruction.

This week reflects on how you already lead simply by living. You may not notice the seeds you plant, but others feel them.

Let your presence be your teaching. Let your life be your leadership.

Day 1: Leadership Begins Within

The Hidden Pattern:

Gentle leadership starts with how you lead yourself. Your inner alignment shapes the energy you bring to every interaction.

The Sacred Reframe:

You do not need a title to be a leader. Every soul you touch is influenced by how you live.

The Devoted Practice:

Whisper: *"I lead with my life."*

Journal: *Where am I already quietly influencing others through how I live? What inner shift would strengthen that influence?*

Optional: Choose one intentional action today that models what you value.

Day 2: Leading Without Control

The Hidden Pattern:

True leadership is not about control; it's about inspiration. People are moved more by example than by force.

The Sacred Reframe:

You can invite, encourage, and model—but you do not have to control outcomes. Leadership trusts the process in others.

The Devoted Practice:

Whisper: *"I inspire, I do not control."*

Journal: *Where am I trying to force someone to change? What would it look like to simply embody what I hope to see?*

Optional: Release control by writing: *"I trust their path."*

Day 3: The Power of Quiet Influence

The Hidden Pattern:

You may never know how much your quiet integrity inspires others. Leadership often happens in ways you cannot measure.

The Sacred Reframe:

You do not need recognition to make a difference. The way you live is already planting seeds.

The Devoted Practice:

Whisper: *"My life is a living prayer."*

Journal: *Who has quietly influenced me by how they live? What seed might I be planting through my own life right now?*

Optional: Write a note of gratitude (even if you don't send it) to someone who has influenced you.

Day 4: Leadership Through Kindness

The Hidden Pattern:

Kindness is one of the most powerful forms of leadership. It softens tension, builds trust, and opens hearts.

The Sacred Reframe:

Every kind word or gesture is an invitation for others to rise into love.

The Devoted Practice:

Whisper: *"My kindness changes things."*

Journal: *When have I been deeply changed by someone's kindness? How can I offer that today?*

Optional: Do one unexpected kind thing for someone without mentioning it.

Day 5: Humility as Strength

The Hidden Pattern:

Gentle leadership is rooted in humility, not ego. The strongest leaders are willing to listen, learn, and admit when they are wrong.

The Sacred Reframe:

Humility does not make you weak; it makes you trustworthy. It shows others that growth is safe.

The Devoted Practice:

Whisper: *"I lead with humility and grace."*

Journal: *Where have I been afraid to admit I was wrong? How might humility strengthen my influence?*

Optional: Offer a quiet apology or acknowledgment where needed today.

Day 6: Leading With Love, Not Fear

The Hidden Pattern:

Leadership rooted in fear pushes. Leadership rooted in love invites.

The Sacred Reframe:

You are not here to scare people into growth; you are here to embody love so fully that they feel safe to grow around you.

The Devoted Practice:

Whisper: *"Love is my leadership."*

Journal: *Where do I still lead with fear or urgency? How can I shift to leading with love instead?*

Optional: Visualize yourself radiating love like a soft light as you move through your day.

Day 7: The Legacy of Gentle Leadership

The Hidden Pattern:

Gentle leadership lasts because it touches hearts, not just behaviors. The seeds you plant now may bloom long after you are gone.

The Sacred Reframe:

You are already leaving a legacy through every quiet act of love and truth. That is enough.

The Devoted Practice:

Light a candle and whisper: *"May my life bless others long after I am gone."*

Journal: *What kind of legacy do I want to leave? What small acts this week felt like seeds of that legacy?*

Optional: Write a one-sentence blessing for those who will be touched by your life, even if you never meet them.

WEEK 6: SACRED LISTENING —
BECOMING A SAFE SPACE

"The quieter you become, the more you can hear." – Ram Dass

Listening is more than hearing words—it is receiving a soul.

Sacred listening requires patience, humility, and openness. It means quieting your inner response long enough to hold another's truth without judgment or interruption.

We live in a world starved for safe spaces. When someone feels listened to deeply, they encounter healing without even realizing it.

Your willingness to be present, to lean in, and to listen with your whole self can be the sanctuary someone needs.

This week, notice when you are tempted to rush into advice or answers. Instead, soften. Listen longer.

Let silence stretch. Trust that your quiet attention is a gift of love.

Day 1: Listening Creates Sanctuary

The Hidden Pattern:

When you truly listen, you create a space where another soul can rest. Listening is not waiting to speak—it's making room for someone's truth.

The Sacred Reframe:

Your presence can feel like shelter to others when you listen with your whole being.

The Devoted Practice:

Whisper: *"I am a safe space."*

Journal: *When have I felt most safe to speak my truth? What made that space feel safe?*

Optional: Sit with someone today and listen without interrupting or giving advice.

Day 2: Listening Without Agenda

The Hidden Pattern:

We often listen to respond, to fix, or to relate. Sacred listening has no agenda; it simply receives.

The Sacred Reframe:

You do not need to solve anything. Receiving someone's words fully is a gift in itself.

The Devoted Practice:

Whisper: *"I listen to understand, not to reply."*

Journal: *Where do I feel tempted to jump in or fix? How can I release that and just listen?*

Optional: Practice this with yourself: write a stream-of-consciousness journal entry, then read it back as if listening to a dear friend.

Day 3: Hearing Between the Words

The Hidden Pattern:

Sacred listening is not just to words—it's to tone, pauses, and what's left unsaid. Souls speak in many ways.

The Sacred Reframe:

When you listen deeply, you hear more than stories—you hear hearts.

The Devoted Practice:

Whisper: *"I listen with my whole self."*

Journal: *Who in my life might be saying more in silence than in words? What might they need me to feel, not just hear?*

Optional: Spend five minutes in silence with someone or in nature, attuning to the unspoken.

Day 4: Listening to Yourself

The Hidden Pattern:

You cannot be a safe space for others if you ignore your own voice. Self-listening is the foundation of sacred listening.

The Sacred Reframe:

When you honor your own needs, you model trust and presence for others. Listening inward teaches others it's safe to listen to themselves.

The Devoted Practice:

Whisper: *"My voice matters too."*

Journal: *What have I been trying to tell myself lately? What do I need to hear from me?*

Optional: Sit quietly with your hand over your heart and ask: *"What do you need from me right now?"* Write whatever comes.

Day 5: Silence as Healing

The Hidden Pattern:

Sometimes the most healing thing you can offer is silence.
Sacred listening allows others to unfold without rushing them.

The Sacred Reframe:

Silence is not absence; it is presence without pressure. It tells
someone: *"You are safe to take your time."*

The Devoted Practice:

Whisper: *"Silence can be love."*

Journal: *When has silence felt healing for me? Who might need
my patient silence now?*

Optional: Sit in silence for five minutes, imagining
yourself holding someone in gentle love.

Day 6: Protecting What You Hear

The Hidden Pattern:

What others share with you is sacred. Protecting their words is a form of holy trust.

The Sacred Reframe:

When you hold someone's truth with respect and confidentiality, you show them they are worthy of care.

The Devoted Practice:

Whisper: *"I hold their words as sacred."*

Journal: *Who has trusted me with their truth? How can I honor that trust even more deeply?*

Optional: Light a candle in gratitude for the trust others place in you.

Day 7: Becoming a Safe Space

The Hidden Pattern:

A safe space is not perfect—it's present. It's a heart that welcomes without judgment.

The Sacred Reframe:

You don't need specific skills to be a healer. Your steady presence and compassionate listening are already medicine.

The Devoted Practice:

Light a candle and whisper: *"May I be a safe space for others and for myself."*

Journal: *What did I learn this week about listening? How do I feel when I am fully listened to?*

Optional: Write a blessing for the people who feel safe with you, even if you never share it.

WEEK 7: PRESENCE IN MOTION — MAKING THE MUNDANE HOLY

"There are no ordinary moments. Every moment is sacred." –
Dan Millman

Sacredness does not live only in ritual or set-apart spaces; it pulses in every ordinary moment.

Washing dishes, pouring coffee, walking down the street— all of it can become holy when approached with reverence. Presence transforms the mundane into prayer.

Every movement offers an invitation: will you rush through it, or will you let it become sacred? Folding laundry becomes a blessing of care. Cooking dinner becomes communion. Breathing in the morning light becomes prayer.

This week, choose one small daily action and slow it down. Notice its textures, sounds, and rhythms.

Treat it as holy. In doing so, you'll remember: there are no ordinary moments.

All of life is sacred ground.

Day 1: The Sacred in Small Things

The Hidden Pattern:

Sacredness does not live only in ritual; it lives in how you approach the smallest tasks. Every movement can be a prayer.

The Sacred Reframe:

When you treat the ordinary with reverence, you remind yourself that all of life is holy ground.

The Devoted Practice:

Whisper: *"Nothing is too small to be sacred."*

Journal: *What simple action today could I approach as holy?*

Optional: Choose one daily task—pouring coffee, folding laundry—and do it slowly, with full attention.

Day 2: The Prayer of Movement

The Hidden Pattern:

The body speaks devotion through motion. Walking, sweeping, or stirring can all become moving meditations.

The Sacred Reframe:

When you move with presence, you pray with your body, even without words.

The Devoted Practice:

Whisper: *"My body moves as prayer."*

Journal: *What movements in my daily life feel most calming or intentional? How can I bring more awareness to them?*

Optional: Take a slow, mindful walk today, noticing each step as an offering.

Day 3: Cleaning as Clearing

The Hidden Pattern:

Tidying, washing, or clearing spaces can shift energy. Cleaning is not just maintenance—it's making room for new life.

The Sacred Reframe:

You are not just scrubbing surfaces; you are blessing them, making space for what nourishes you.

The Devoted Practice:

Whisper: *"I clear space to welcome the sacred."*

Journal: *What space feels heavy or stagnant? How would clearing it feel like love for myself?*

Optional: Choose one small space to clear intentionally today, whispering gratitude as you do.

Day 4: Eating as Devotion

The Hidden Pattern:

Every meal is a chance to honor the body and the earth that nourishes it. Eating with presence turns food into gratitude.

The Sacred Reframe:

When you slow down and savor, you transform a basic act into holy communion with life.

The Devoted Practice:

Whisper before eating: *"Thank you for this nourishment."*

Journal: *How do I usually approach meals? What shifts when I eat with gratitude?*

Optional: Prepare or eat one meal today slowly, savoring each bite as an act of devotion.

Day 5: Working as Offering

The Hidden Pattern:

Whatever you do—whether for a paycheck, a home, or a dream —can be offered with love. Work becomes sacred when done with intention.

The Sacred Reframe:

You are not just completing tasks; you are contributing your energy to the world.

The Devoted Practice:

Whisper: *"May my work bless someone today."*

Journal: *What parts of my work feel draining? What parts could I reframe as an offering?*

Optional: Dedicate one task today as an act of service, even if no one knows.

Day 6: The Art of Pausing

The Hidden Pattern:

Sacred motion includes sacred stillness. Pausing between actions reminds you that you are not just doing—you are being.

The Sacred Reframe:

A single conscious breath can transform your entire day into presence.

The Devoted Practice:

Whisper: *"Even my pauses are holy."*

Journal: *Where can I add small pauses today to remember I am more than my tasks?*

Optional: Take three conscious breaths before starting or ending each task.

Day 7: Living as Devotion

The Hidden Pattern:

When you bring presence to motion, every part of life becomes an altar.

The Sacred Reframe:

You don't need to escape daily life to be spiritual—your life itself is the practice.

The Devoted Practice:

Light a candle and whisper: *"My life is my devotion."*

Journal: *What simple actions felt most sacred this week? What will I carry forward as daily prayer?*

Optional: Write a blessing for your daily routine, thanking it for shaping your soul.

WEEK 8: LEADING WITH LOVE — COURAGE WITHOUT CONTROL

"Love is the bridge between you and everything." – Rumi

Fear often disguises itself as control—the urge to direct outcomes, manage people, or holding tightly to what we cannot change.

Love, by contrast, trusts. It loosens its grip and makes space for growth, even when outcomes remain uncertain.

Leading with love is courageous. It means stepping back when fear wants to push forward. It means trusting Spirit to weave what you cannot see. Love creates freedom, while control creates tension.

The most lasting influence you will ever carry comes not from grasping but from releasing.

This week, notice where fear tempts you to control. Ask: what would love choose here? Then, try loosening your grip—even slightly.

Let love lead.

Day 1: Love Over Fear

The Hidden Pattern:

Fear wants to control. Love trusts. Leadership through love allows others to grow at their own pace.

The Sacred Reframe:

When you release the need to control outcomes, you make space for Spirit to work. Love is a greater teacher than fear will ever be.

The Devoted Practice:

Whisper: *"I choose love over control."*

Journal: *Where am I trying to force an outcome? How would love respond differently?*

Optional: Place your hand over your heart and take three slow breaths, imagining love softening your grip.

Day 2: The Courage to Step Back

The Hidden Pattern:

Sometimes the bravest thing you can do is step back and let someone find their own way.

The Sacred Reframe:

Trusting others does not mean abandoning them; it means believing in their strength.

The Devoted Practice:

Whisper: *"I trust their strength and path."*

Journal: *Who am I trying to protect by stepping in too much? What would trusting them look like?*

Optional: Light a candle for them and speak their name with a blessing instead of trying to direct them.

Day 3: Holding Space Without Fixing

The Hidden Pattern:

True love holds space for discomfort without rushing to "fix" it. Healing happens in safety, not in control.

The Sacred Reframe:

Your presence can be more healing than any advice. You are not responsible for their outcomes, only your love.

The Devoted Practice:

Whisper: *"My love is enough without fixing."*

Journal: *Where have I felt pressure to fix? What might it feel like to just hold space instead?*

Optional: Practice sitting silently with someone or holding them in loving thought without words.

Day 4: Softening the Urge to Push

The Hidden Pattern:

Love invites; fear pushes. When you push, others resist. When you invite, hearts open.

The Sacred Reframe:

It takes courage to release the need for urgency. Trust that timing unfolds as it should.

The Devoted Practice:

Whisper: *"I invite, I do not push."*

Journal: *Where do I feel urgency in someone else's journey? How can I soften that today?*

Optional: Breathe slowly whenever you feel the need to push; repeat the mantra above.

Day 5: Letting Spirit Lead

The Hidden Pattern:

You are not meant to carry the full weight of others' paths. Spirit is already leading them, even when you can't see it.

The Sacred Reframe:

You are a companion, not the guide. Trusting Spirit's role frees you to love without fear.

The Devoted Practice:

Whisper: *"Spirit leads; I love."*

Journal: *Where do I need to let Spirit do the guiding instead of me?*

Optional: Write a short prayer asking Spirit to guide someone you care for.

Day 6: Courage in Love's Patience

The Hidden Pattern:

Patience is not passivity—it is love's courage. It trusts that growth takes time.

The Sacred Reframe:

Waiting with love is harder than acting with control, but it is more powerful.

The Devoted Practice:

Whisper: *"I am patient because I love."*

Journal: *Where is patience being asked of me right now?*

Optional: Take one slow, deliberate action today as an act of patient love.

Day 7: Love Is Enough

The Hidden Pattern:

You do not need to have the right words, the perfect plan, or all the answers. Love itself is enough.

The Sacred Reframe:

When you love with openness, you are already a leader. That is your sacred gift.

The Devoted Practice:

Light a candle and whisper: *"My love is enough."*

Journal: *What did I learn about love and control this week? How did letting go feel in my body?*

Optional: Write a blessing for those you are learning to love without trying to control.

WEEK 9: DAILY DEVOTION — SMALL ACTS OF ALIGNMENT

"Great things are done by a series of small things brought together." – Vincent van Gogh

Transformation rarely arrives in dramatic waves; it is built through the quiet rhythm of daily acts.

A whispered prayer. A journal entry. A mindful breath. The accumulation of these small acts creates a life of alignment.

There is power in small things. Each time you return to your practice—even imperfectly—you are shaping your soul. Each repetition carves a groove of devotion that grows deeper with time.

The strength of your becoming is in the steady, quiet return.

This week, focus not on doing something grand but on one consistent act. Water the seed. Return to the breath. Light the candle.

These small devotions will become the foundation of your sacred life.

Day 1: The Sacred Power
of Small Things

The Hidden Pattern:

The soul changes through consistent, quiet devotion. It's the small, repeated acts—not the rare grand ones—that shape who you are becoming.

The Sacred Reframe:

You don't need to move mountains today; you need to place one stone of devotion, again and again.

The Devoted Practice:

Whisper: *"My small acts matter."*

Journal: *What small habit has been shaping me lately, for better or worse? How can I make it more intentional?*

Optional: Choose one small, nourishing habit to repeat today with intention.

Day 2: Aligning With What Matters

The Hidden Pattern:

When your small actions match your values, your soul rests easier. Alignment builds trust in yourself.

The Sacred Reframe:

Each choice is a prayer. Every aligned action whispers, *"This is who I am becoming."*

The Devoted Practice:

Whisper: *"Every choice can be sacred."*

Journal: *What value do I want to live by today? What is one action that would align with it?*

Optional: Write the chosen value on a sticky note or card and keep it visible.

Day 3: Devotion in Daily Tasks

The Hidden Pattern:

Folding laundry, answering emails, brushing your teeth—every task can carry sacred energy when done with presence.

The Sacred Reframe:

Devotion is not just prayer or meditation; it's how you approach every ordinary action with love.

The Devoted Practice:

Whisper: *"Even this is holy."*

Journal: *Which daily task feels like the biggest chore? How could I approach it as devotion?*

Optional: Perform that task slowly today, whispering gratitude as you do.

Day 4: Micro-Alignments Add Up

The Hidden Pattern:

One aligned breath, one kind word, one mindful choice—tiny acts repeated become your spiritual rhythm.

The Sacred Reframe:

You don't need to do everything today; you need to keep doing one small thing at a time.

The Devoted Practice:

Whisper: *"My small steps are sacred."*

Journal: *What three micro-alignments can I choose today to honor my soul?*

Optional: Track them and celebrate at day's end.

Day 5: Devotion Without Perfection

The Hidden Pattern:

Missing a day does not erase your devotion. Returning to alignment is also devotion.

The Sacred Reframe:

You are not behind; every return is sacred. Devotion is measured in love, not flawless consistency.

The Devoted Practice:

Whisper: *"Every return is holy."*

Journal: *Where have I been too harsh on myself for inconsistency? How can I return gently?*

Optional: Light a candle as a symbol of returning, even if imperfectly.

Day 6: Gratitude as Daily Prayer

The Hidden Pattern:

Gratitude anchors devotion. A grateful heart naturally moves toward alignment because it notices what is already sacred.

The Sacred Reframe:

When you give thanks for small things, you train your soul to see the holy in all things.

The Devoted Practice:

Whisper: *"Thank you for this moment."*

Journal: *What three simple things can I thank life for today?*

Optional: Speak your gratitude aloud as you move through your day.

Day 7: Devotion as a Way of Life

The Hidden Pattern:

Daily devotion is not a task to complete; it is a way of being. Every small act becomes a living prayer.

The Sacred Reframe:

Your life is already a sacred offering. When you live aligned, you are devotion itself.

The Devoted Practice:

Light a candle and whisper: *"My life is my prayer."*

Journal: *What daily act felt most devotional this week? How can I keep that rhythm alive?*

Optional: Write a one-sentence blessing for the way you live your ordinary days.

WEEK 10: SOUL RESILIENCE — HOLDING STEADY THROUGH CHANGE

"She stood in the storm, and when the wind did not blow her way, she adjusted her sails." – Elizabeth Edwards

Storms will come, winds will shift, and seasons will turn. Resilience is not built in resisting change, but in rooting deeply enough to bend without breaking.

Like the tree that sways but does not fall, your soul learns to anchor in what cannot be moved.

Resilience doesn't require you to be unshaken.

It allows you to tremble, to weep, to bend, and still remain rooted. It's the strength you build quietly over time, in choosing to stay present to your own soul when life swirls around you.

This week, honor your roots. Remember what has held you through storms before. Breathe into that steady place.

Trust that no matter how strong the winds, your soul is anchored.

Day 1: The Strength Beneath the Surface

The Hidden Pattern:

True resilience is quiet. Like tree roots, it anchors deep below where no one sees.

The Sacred Reframe:

You don't need to appear strong; you need to stay rooted. Strength is built in presence, not performance.

The Devoted Practice:

Whisper: *"I am rooted even in change."*

Journal: *What has kept me standing through past storms? What roots me now?*

Optional: Visualize roots growing from your feet into the earth as you breathe deeply.

Day 2: Flexibility Is Strength

The Hidden Pattern:

Rigid trees snap in fierce winds; flexible ones bend and survive. Resilience is adaptability, not resistance.

The Sacred Reframe:

You are not failing when you change course, you are adjusting your sails.

The Devoted Practice:

Whisper: *"I bend, I do not break."*

Journal: *Where am I resisting change out of fear? What would flexibility look like instead?*

Optional: Stretch or sway gently, imagining your body moving like a tree in the wind.

Day 3: Rest Is Resilience

The Hidden Pattern:

The strongest souls know when to pause. Rest restores the inner reserves needed to keep going.

The Sacred Reframe:

You are not weak for needing rest; you are wise for taking it.

The Devoted Practice:

Whisper: *"Rest is strength."*

Journal: *Where have I been pushing too hard? What rest would feel like love to my body today?*

Optional: Take a short nap, a quiet break, or a moment to simply breathe without doing.

Day 4: Trusting the Storm's Purpose

The Hidden Pattern:

Storms clear what no longer belongs and deepen roots where growth will continue.

The Sacred Reframe:

You are not being punished by change; you are being reshaped. Even in loss, life is rearranging for your good.

The Devoted Practice:

Whisper: *"I trust what the storm is teaching me."*

Journal: *What changes feel hard right now? What wisdom might they be offering?*

Optional: Light a candle and dedicate it as a symbol of hope in the midst of change.

Day 5: The Anchor of Inner Truth

The Hidden Pattern:

When everything shifts outside, inner truth becomes your anchor.

The Sacred Reframe:

You don't need to control every wave; you need to remember who you are in it.

The Devoted Practice:

Whisper: *"My truth holds me steady."*

Journal: *What is one truth I can hold to when everything else feels uncertain?*

Optional: Write that truth on a card or paper to carry with you today.

Day 6: Courage to Keep Showing Up

The Hidden Pattern:

Resilience is not about never falling; it's about rising again and again. Courage is often just choosing to show up one more time.

The Sacred Reframe:

You are stronger than you realize. Every time you return to life after being knocked down, you expand your soul's capacity.

The Devoted Practice:

Whisper: *"I keep showing up."*

Journal: *Where in my life do I feel like giving up? What would showing up gently look like instead?*

Optional: Take one small action today to move forward, no matter how tiny.

Day 7: The Blessing of What You've Survived

The Hidden Pattern:

Every challenge you've survived has shaped the strength you carry now.

The Sacred Reframe:

You are not fragile; you are sacredly strong. Honor what you've survived by blessing the resilience it gave you.

The Devoted Practice:

Light a candle and whisper: *"I bless my resilience."*

Journal: *What am I proud of surviving? What strength do I carry now because of it?*

Optional: Write a blessing to your past self who kept going.

WEEK 11: LIVING LEGACY — PLANTING SEEDS THROUGH ACTION

"Carve your name on hearts, not tombstones. A legacy is etched into the minds of others and the stories they share about you." –
Shannon L. Alder

Legacy is not something far off in the future; it is being written now in every interaction, every gesture, every word.

Today the way you live plants seeds that will outlast you, shaping the soil of tomorrow.

You may never see all the fruit of what you plant, but trust that it matters. A kind word can echo through generations. A steady choice can ripple outward in ways you'll never fully know.

Your legacy is not someday—it is this day.

This week, notice the seeds you are planting through your presence. Be intentional with them.

Choose kindness, choose truth, choose love. These are the seeds that endure.

Day 1: Legacy Begins Now

The Hidden Pattern:

Legacy is not something you leave behind someday; it's something you create daily with the way you live.

The Sacred Reframe:

Your words, gestures, and choices are planting seeds in others right now—whether you see them grow or not.

The Devoted Practice:

Whisper: *"I plant seeds with every action."*

Journal: *What seeds am I planting with the way I live now? What do I hope will grow from them?*

Optional: Hold a seed, stone, or small token while whispering gratitude for the life you're shaping.

Day 2: Small Seeds, Great Impact

The Hidden Pattern:

A single smile, kind word, or act of patience can ripple further than you imagine.

The Sacred Reframe:

You don't have to do something grand to matter. The smallest seeds often grow the strongest roots.

The Devoted Practice:

Whisper: *"My small kindness shapes the world."*

Journal: *Who has planted a small but lasting seed in me? What small kindness can I offer today?*

Optional: Perform one quiet, intentional act of kindness with no expectation of acknowledgment.

Day 3: Living What You Want to Leave

The Hidden Pattern:

The life you live now teaches others what is possible. Every choice models something.

The Sacred Reframe:

If you want to leave love, joy, or courage behind, you must live them now.

The Devoted Practice:

Whisper: *"I live the legacy I want to leave."*

Journal: *What qualities do I hope people remember about me? How can I embody them today?*

Optional: Write one word that represents your legacy and keep it visible this week.

Day 4: Planting Through Presence

The Hidden Pattern:

Sometimes the greatest gift you can leave someone is how you made them feel when you were with them.

The Sacred Reframe:

Being fully present plants seeds of trust and love that may last a lifetime.

The Devoted Practice:

Whisper: *"My presence plants love."*

Journal: *Who in my life feels safe and seen when I am present with them? How can I offer more of that presence?*

Optional: Dedicate extra time today to truly listen or be present with one person.

Day 5: Tending What You've Planted

The Hidden Pattern:

Seeds need tending. Relationships, dreams, and values flourish when watered with consistency.

The Sacred Reframe:

Legacy is not just what you start; it's what you nurture over time.

The Devoted Practice:

Whisper: *"I tend what matters."*

Journal: *What relationships or values need more of my attention to grow strong?*

Optional: Write a message, make a call, or take one step to nurture something important today.

Day 6: Trusting Seeds You'll Never See Bloom

The Hidden Pattern:

Some of the most meaningful seeds you plant will bloom long after you are gone.

The Sacred Reframe:

You may never see the full impact of your life—and that's okay. Love plants without needing proof.

The Devoted Practice:

Whisper: *"I plant for a future I may never see."*

Journal: *What have I been doing that might bless someone long after today?*

Optional: Light a candle for future generations and whisper a blessing over them.

Day 7: Blessing Your Living Legacy

The Hidden Pattern:

Your life already carries a legacy—through the people you've touched, the love you've given, and the truth you've lived.

The Sacred Reframe:

You don't have to become someone different to leave a legacy; you already are one.

The Devoted Practice:

Light a candle and whisper: *"May my life bless the world."*

Journal: *What legacy am I already leaving in small ways? What do I want to deepen?*

Optional: Write a blessing to your future self, thanking them for continuing to plant love through action.

WEEK 12: THE PRACTICE OF PEACE — STILLNESS AS STRENGTH

"Peace is not the absence of chaos, but the presence of calm in the midst of it." – Unknown

Peace is not found in the absence of chaos but in the choice to anchor calm within it.

Life will not always quiet itself for you—but you can return to the stillness that already lives inside you.

Peace is a practice. It grows stronger each time you return, even in the midst of noise, even in the presence of storms.

This is strength—not to avoid life's mess, but to remain rooted in calm through it.

This week, give yourself permission to pause. Breathe. Choose stillness, even briefly. Let this quiet be your strength.

The more you practice, the more peace will become your natural way of being.

Day 1: Peace Is a Practice

The Hidden Pattern:

Peace is not something you find—it's something you cultivate. Like any practice, it grows stronger the more you return to it.

The Sacred Reframe:

You do not need to escape life to find peace; you only need to pause and choose it, moment by moment.

The Devoted Practice:

Whisper: *"I can practice peace right now."*

Journal: *What practices help me feel calm even in chaos? How can I return to them more often?*

Optional: Take three slow, deep breaths whenever you feel rushed today.

Day 2: Stillness as Strength

The Hidden Pattern:

Stillness is not weakness; it is the strength to pause instead of reacting.

The Sacred Reframe:

Choosing stillness when everything calls for urgency is an act of courage. It allows you to respond from wisdom, not fear.

The Devoted Practice:

Whisper: *"My stillness is my strength."*

Journal: *Where do I react too quickly? What would happen if I paused first?*

Optional: Pause for one full breath before answering anyone today.

Day 3: Breathing as Anchor

The Hidden Pattern:

The breath is the simplest, most reliable anchor to peace. Returning to it is returning to yourself.

The Sacred Reframe:

No matter what happens around you, your breath reminds you: you are here, alive, and safe in this moment.

The Devoted Practice:

Whisper: *"Peace is in my breath."*

Journal: *When do I forget to breathe deeply? How does my body feel when I remember?*

Optional: Practice box breathing—inhale 4, hold 4, exhale 4, hold 4—for five rounds.

Day 4: Choosing Peace Over Proving

The Hidden Pattern:

Much of our unrest comes from trying to prove ourselves. Peace begins where proving ends.

The Sacred Reframe:

You don't need to win every argument, finish every task, or please every person. Peace is letting go of the need to be right or perfect.

The Devoted Practice:

Whisper: *"I choose peace over proving."*

Journal: *Where am I trying to prove something right now? What would peace look like instead?*

Optional: Release one task or argument today that doesn't truly matter.

Day 5: Creating Calm Spaces

The Hidden Pattern:

Your environment affects your inner world. Peace grows where your surroundings feel clear and welcoming.

The Sacred Reframe:

Even a small corner of calm—a tidy desk, a lit candle—can remind your soul to settle.

The Devoted Practice:

Whisper: *"I create space for peace."*

Journal: *What part of my space feels heavy or chaotic? How can I bring a little more calm to it today?*

Optional: Light a candle or clear one small area with intention, saying the mantra above.

Day 6: Protecting Your Peace

The Hidden Pattern:

Peace is precious and must sometimes be protected.
Boundaries guard the calm you've worked to create.

The Sacred Reframe:

You are allowed to say no to chaos, even if others don't
understand. Protecting your peace is protecting your soul.

The Devoted Practice:

Whisper: *"My peace is sacred."*

Journal: *Who or what disrupts my peace most often? What
boundary would honor me?*

Optional: Write one loving boundary to hold today, even in a
small way.

Day 7: The Blessing of Inner Calm

The Hidden Pattern:

Peace is a gift you give yourself, but it also blesses everyone around you. Calm energy is contagious.

The Sacred Reframe:

The more you cultivate inner calm, the more you quietly lead others toward it too.

The Devoted Practice:

Light a candle and whisper: *"May my peace bless the world."*

Journal: *What moments of peace stood out this week? How can I carry this calm into next week?*

Optional: Write a simple blessing for your own heart, thanking it for learning peace.

WEEK 13: INTEGRATION —
THE DEVOTED LIFE

"How you live each day is how you live your life." – Annie Dillard

Integration is the weaving together of everything you have practiced.

It is the recognition that your devotion has not been about becoming someone new, it has been about embodying who you already are.

Each small act, each return, each quiet choice has brought you here. This is the devoted life: living aligned with love, truth, and presence in every ordinary day.

Integration is not an ending but a deepening. It is becoming more fully yourself.

This week, celebrate how far you have come. Honor the practices that now live in you. And remember: the life you live each day is your truest devotion.

Keep walking it with presence, and your soul will continue to blossom.

Day 1: Becoming What You Practice

The Hidden Pattern:

Your life is shaped by what you practice daily. Habits of presence, kindness, and truth eventually become who you are.

The Sacred Reframe:

You are not becoming someone new; you are embodying the truest version of yourself through repeated love.

The Devoted Practice:

Whisper: *"I become what I practice."*

Journal: *What practices have been shaping me this season? What am I proud to be becoming?*

Optional: Light a candle and thank yourself for showing up, even imperfectly.

Day 2: Living Your Values in Motion

The Hidden Pattern:

Values are not beliefs you hold in your head; they are truths you live with your hands and feet.

The Sacred Reframe:

Every decision you make, big or small, is a chance to embody your values. Integration is living them, not just naming them.

The Devoted Practice:

Whisper: *"My life shows what I believe."*

Journal: *What value matters most to me right now? How can I embody it in a visible way today?*

Optional: Write that value on paper and keep it somewhere you will see often.

Day 3: Bringing Spirit into the Ordinary

The Hidden Pattern:

Integration is not about adding more rituals; it's about inviting Spirit into what you already do—walking, cooking, speaking.

The Sacred Reframe:

Your life is already holy when you live it with intention.

The Devoted Practice:

Whisper: *"Spirit moves through everything I do."*

Journal: *What daily habit could feel more sacred if I invited Spirit into it?*

Optional: Dedicate one ordinary task today as an offering of love.

Day 4: The Devotion of Returning

The Hidden Pattern:

You will wander. You will forget. Integration is not about never straying—it's about gently returning every time you do.

The Sacred Reframe:

Each return to alignment strengthens your devotion. Love lives in the coming back.

The Devoted Practice:

Whisper: *"I return again and again."*

Journal: *What practice or truth do I want to return to more consistently?*

Optional: Light a candle as a symbol of returning to your path today.

Day 5: Your Presence as Offering

The Hidden Pattern:

You don't have to wait for the "right time" to give your gifts. Your presence, lived with integrity and love, is already a sacred offering.

The Sacred Reframe:

Your life blesses others not because it's perfect, but because it's honest and wholehearted.

The Devoted Practice:

Whisper: *"My presence is my offering."*

Journal: *Who might be blessed simply by me showing up authentically?*

Optional: Offer your presence fully to one person or task today as if it were a gift.

Day 6: The Devoted Life Is Gentle

The Hidden Pattern:

Integration does not mean rushing or striving; it means quietly weaving love into the fabric of your days.

The Sacred Reframe:

Your spiritual life is not separate from your ordinary life—it is how you live it, slowly and with care.

The Devoted Practice:

Whisper: *"Gentleness is devotion."*

Journal: *Where can I soften my approach to life today while staying devoted to what matters?*

Optional: Move through one task today at half your normal speed, breathing as you go.

Day 7: The Blessing of a Devoted Life

The Hidden Pattern:

A devoted life is not a life of perfection but of presence. It is a life where love, truth, and Spirit move quietly through every choice.

The Sacred Reframe:

You are already living your devotion, one honest step at a time. That is enough.

The Devoted Practice:

Light a candle and whisper: *"My life is my devotion."*

Journal: *What has shifted in me through this journey of devoted presence? What rhythms feel like home now?*

Optional: Write a short blessing for the life you are building, thanking it for becoming your prayer.

THE FLAMEKEEPER'S WHISPER

"The smallest flame, tended with love, lights the longest night."
– Unknown

You have moved from shadow to sacred, from repatterning to presence. This is where devotion becomes who you are—not just what you do.

May your life be a quiet prayer, your love a steady flame, and your presence a gift to every soul you meet. Blessed are you, Flamekeeper. You carry the sacred in your ordinary moments, and that is holy work.

You have walked the path of *Devoted Presence*. Through 90 days of small acts, quiet prayers, and lived truth, you have become more than someone who seeks devotion—you have become a keeper of it.

Every choice you make now carries a quiet weight. Your life whispers of Spirit not because you speak it loudly, but because you live it honestly.

You are no longer simply a seeker; you are what the Spirit calls **Flamekeeper**—one who tends the ember of love and truth not only for yourself but for the world.

A Reflection

What does it mean to me to be a Flamekeeper? Where in my life am I tending quiet flames for others, even without realizing it?

The Offering of Presence: When the Soul Becomes the Gift

"Your presence is your power. Your story is your legacy. And your becoming… is the offering." — Unknown

Final Devoted Practice: "The Legacy Light"

You will need:

- A white candle or tealight
- A small bowl of water
- A pen and small paper

Light the candle and whisper: "I am here. I have arrived."

Hold the bowl of water and say:

"I bless the path behind me. I bless the path before me. And I bless the offering I now become."

Write a one-line soul truth you want to carry into the next chapter. Fold the paper and hold it between both palms.

Close your eyes and say:

"May my life be my prayer. May my truth be my offering. May my presence be my legacy."

Place the folded paper in a sacred place or altar space.

The Path Is Lit Within Me

I do not walk behind the sacred—I carry it.

I do not wait for worth—I embody it.

I do not question the voice—I become it.

This soul, this life, this breath—

Let the world be changed by presence.

Let the path be lit from within.

You have lived your devotion — not in grand gestures, but in sacred presence. You have honored your truth, tended your inner flame, and become a quiet source of light in the lives around you.

Now, the path opens toward a sacred offering.
Not because you must — but because you *can*.

Legacy is a love letter to the life you offer back.
It is the way you speak with your presence, lead with your integrity, and pass on your healing.
It is not about leaving something behind —
it is about living forward with intention.

Let your life become a gift.
Let your legacy begin every day.

The next volume is not about learning; it is about offering.
It will ask you to step forward—not loudly, but faithfully—
offering the quiet medicine of your life to the world.

Final Prompt:

What would it look like to give from the soul—not out of obligation, but out of overflow?

TOWARD LEGACY

You have walked into *Devoted Presence* — learning not only to see differently, but to live differently. Presence is not perfection; it is showing up with your whole self, steady and true, in the ordinary rhythms of each day.

Yet devotion, once embodied, longs to be offered.

Presence begins within, but legacy flows outward. What we carry becomes what we share. What we live becomes what we leave behind.

The next season of this journey is *Devoted Legacy*. Here, the focus shifts from the inward to the outward, from becoming to offering.

Through **Reflection**, you will pause and remember what your life has carried.

Through **Sacred Reframe**, you will see with mercy what once felt like a burden.

Through **Devoted Action — your Sacred Offering**, you will take steps that embody love, truth, and service.

Through **Legacy Practice**, you will anchor these acts into rhythm, so that what you live each day becomes the story you leave behind.

ACKNOWLEDGMENTS

To the quiet mornings, the unnoticed offerings, and the daily return to truth — you became my temple.

To the teachers of stillness and the ones who show up without fanfare — your lives inspired this volume more than you may know.

To those who hold spiritual spaces with integrity and softness — thank you for modeling what it means to lead with presence.

And to the sacred spark that keeps calling me deeper — this work is in your honor.